AF588271

THE MAKING OF AVATAR

KENNY ABDO

Fly!
An Imprint of Abdo Zoom
abdobooks.com

abdobooks.com

Published by Abdo Zoom, a division of ABDO, P.O. Box 398166, Minneapolis, Minnesota 55439.

Printed in the United States of America, North Mankato, Minnesota.
052023
092023

Photo Credits: Alamy, AP Images, Everett Collection, Getty Images, Shutterstock
Production Contributors: Kenny Abdo, Jennie Forsberg, Grace Hansen
Design Contributors: Candice Keimig, Neil Klinepier, Colleen McLaren

Library of Congress Control Number: 2022946935

Publisher's Cataloging-in-Publication Data

Names: Abdo, Kenny, author.
Title: The making of Avatar / by Kenny Abdo
Description: Minneapolis, Minnesota : Abdo Zoom, 2024 | Series: Blockbusters | Includes online resources and index.
Identifiers: ISBN 9781098281281 (lib. bdg.) | ISBN 9781098281984 (ebook) | ISBN 9781098282332 (Read-to-me ebook)
Subjects: LCSH: Motion pictures--Juvenile literature. | Filmmaking (Motion pictures)--Juvenile literature. | Avatar (Motion picture : 2009)--Juvenile literature. | Motion pictures--Production and direction--Juvenile literature.
Classification: DDC 791.43--dc23

TABLE OF CONTENTS

AVATAR

Through groundbreaking technology and clever storytelling, *Avatar* whisked audiences away to a whole new world!

As one of the most expensive movies ever made, fans fell in love with the Na'vi tribe and their home planet of Pandora.

LIGHTS, CAMERA, ...

Director James Cameron made a name for himself by creating some of the most beloved movies of all time! Including huge blockbusters like *Terminator 2: Judgement Day* and *Titanic*.

Cameron had the idea for *Avatar* in the 1990s. However, he felt like **CGI** was not advanced enough yet. After seeing *Lord of the Rings* in 2001, Cameron knew the time was right.

ACTION!

While writing the film, Cameron was inspired by every science fiction book he had read as a kid. He also wanted to explore themes about the environment, **colonization**, and technology.

Cameron developed a new 3D camera system for *Avatar*. The technology helped him capture something audiences had never seen before!

Linguist Dr. Paul Frommer was hired to create the Na'vi language. Frommer developed more than 1,000 words for the actors to speak to sound otherworldly!

Avatar took four years to make. That's twice as long as most Hollywood movies! But all the hard work paid off.

LEGACY

Avatar is the highest **grossing** film in movie history. It is the first film to make more than 2 billion dollars. *Avatar* won many awards including three **Oscars**!

Avatar: The Way of the Water was released in 2022. Three more **sequels** were also announced, guaranteeing fans more time with their favorite Na'vi while exploring new parts of Pandora!

GLOSSARY

CGI – short for computer-generated imagery. Artists use CGI to create a 3D depiction of an object, environment, or living creature. CGI can also add images to a live action shot.

colonization – when one country takes control of another country or region while forming a settlement to control the area and take the resources.

grossing – producing or earning an amount of money.

linguist – a person who studies languages.

Oscar – another name for an Academy Award. It is one of several awards the Academy of Motion Picture Arts and Sciences gives annually to achievement in the movie industry.

sequel – a movie or other work that continues the story begun in an earlier work.

ONLINE RESOURCES

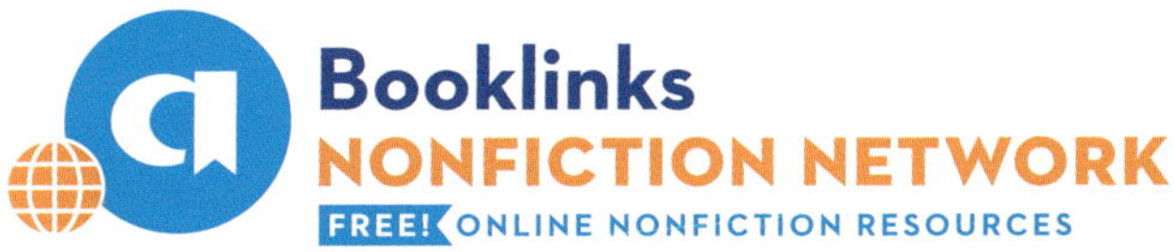

To learn more about the making of *Avatar*, please visit **abdobooklinks.com** or scan this QR code. These links are routinely monitored and updated to provide the most current information available.

INDEX